D0761659

For the ones I love, Cathy, Claire, Maddy, and Tom — L.A.

First edition for the United States and Canada published in 2012
by Barron's Educational Series, Inc.

Original edition copyright ©2012 by Frances Lincoln Limited.
Text and illustrations copyright ©2012 by Laurence Anholt.

Illustrated with watercolors.
Set in Zenke Hand and Bembo.

Visit the Anholt website www.anholt.co.uk.

All rights reserved.
No part of this publication may be reproduced or distributed in any form or by any means
without the written permission of the copyright owner.

All inquiries should be addressed to:
Barron's Educational Series, Inc.
250 Wireless Boulevard
Hauppauge, New York 11788
www.barronseduc.com

ISBN: 978-1-4380-0114-2
Library of Congress Control Number: 2011944290

PHOTOGRAPHIC ACKNOWLEDGMENTS

Page 8, bottom left: *Portrait of Joseph Roulin* (1889) by Vincent van Gogh.
Museum of Modern Art (MOMA), New York (Gift of Mr. and Mrs. William A. M. Burden, Mr. and Mrs. Paul Rosenberg, Nelson A. Rockefeller,
Mr. and Mrs. Armand Bartos, Sidney and Harriet Janis, Mr. and Mrs. Werner E. Josten, and Loula D. Lasker Bequest (by exchange).
196.1989. ©2011. Digital image, The Museum of Modern Art, New York/Scala, Florence.

Page 13: *Self-portrait with a Straw Hat* (probably 1887) by Vincent van Gogh.
(Verso: The Potato Peeler). Metropolitan Museum of Art, New York. Bequest of Miss Adelaide Milton de Groot, 1967.
(Acc.n: 67.187.70a) ©2011. Image copyright The Metropolitan Museum of Art/Art Resource/Scala, Florence.

Page 14, bottom left: *Bull's Head* (1942) by Pablo Picasso.
Musée Picasso, Paris. ©Succession Picasso/DACS, London 2011. White Images/Scala, Florence.

Page 14, bottom right: *Baboon and Young* (Vallauris, 1951) by Pablo Picasso.
Museum of Modern Art (MOMA), New York. Mrs. Simon Guggenheim Fund. 196.1956. ©2011.
©Succession Picasso/DACS, London 2011. Digital image, The Museum of Modern Art, New York/Scala, Florence.

Page 19: *Woman with Baby Carriage* (1950) by Pablo Picasso.
Hirshhorn Museum and Sculpture Garden, Smithsonian Institution. Gift of Joseph H. Hirshhorn, 1972.
©Succession Picasso/DACS, London 2011. Photography by Lee Stalsworth.

Page 23: *Studies of Flying Machine* (Ms. B 2037 f. 80r.) by Leonardo da Vinci.
Institut de France (Bibliothèque), Paris. ©2011. Digital image, Scala, Florence.

Page 29: *Little Dancer of Fourteen Years* (1881) by Edgar Degas.
Musée d'Orsay, Paris. ©2011. White Images/Scala, Florence.

Page 33: *The Codomas*, plate XI from "Jazz" (1943–47) by Henri Matisse.
Museum of Modern Art (MOMA), New York. The Louis E. Stern Collection. Acc. num. 930.1964.11.
©Succession H. Matisse/DACS 2011. Digital image, The Museum of Modern Art, New York/Scala, Florence.

Page 39: *The Rose Path at Giverny* (1920-22) by Claude Monet.
Musée Marmottan, Paris. Photo: akg-images.

Page 43: *Green Apples* (1873) by Paul Cézanne.
Musée d'Orsay, Paris. ©2011. White Images/Scala, Florence.

Date of manufacture: February 2012
Manufactured by: South China Printing, Dongguan, China

9 8 7 6 5 4 3 2 1

Anholt's Artists
ACTIVITY BOOK

Written
and illustrated by

LAURENCE ANHOLT

Contents

The activities in this book are a lot of fun, but you must ask an adult before using sharp or dangerous materials. Activities are carried out at your own risk. The author and publishers disclaim all responsibility for accidents that may occur.

Introduction

Hi there. I'm LAURENCE ANHOLT. I'm an artist and a writer.

In this exciting book, you will meet some of the world's most famous artists. They will teach you how to make your own works of art.

These are not baby activities (like coloring books or painting-by-numbers); these are things you might do at Art School...

You will make proper paintings and sculptures like the ones you see in galleries.

You will also find tips and secrets from people like Vincent van Gogh and Picasso... the heroes of my ANHOLT'S ARTISTS series.

Paint a Portrait with Vincent van Gogh

You will need: large sheets of paper or card stock fixed to a board, a set of water-based paints (like poster paints or acrylics), a paper plate for a palette, brushes and jars of water, an easel if you have one, and lots of courage.

> Hello, my name is Camille. I am very excited because today I will be having a painting lesson with Vincent van Gogh.

> He is working in his studio at the Yellow House....

Vincent is famous for his swirly brushstrokes and bright colors. Some of my favorite paintings are the portraits Vincent made of people he knew... like this picture of my father....

> Ah, my friend, Camille! Are you ready to paint? I'm going to show you how to make a big portrait using lovely colors.

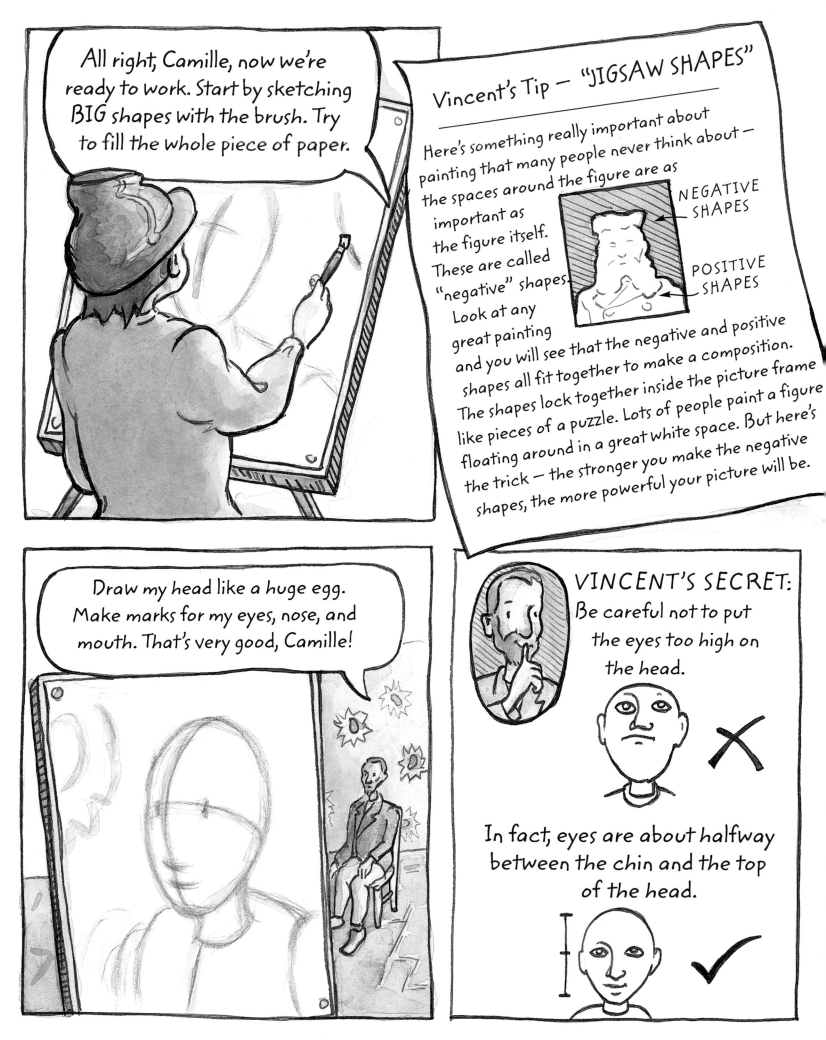

Keep looking at the model all the time. Try squinting your eyes — can you see that one side of the head is dark and one side is light? That's what will make your painting look round and solid as an apple.

When you have covered the whole piece of paper with big bold shapes, it's time to start adding details like the lips, eyes, and ears. Look at my paintings — you will see that I use a small brush and a strong color like blue to draw outlines.

Well done, Camille. That is a wonderful painting! I always sign my pictures. Why don't you sign your own name? It takes a lot of practice to paint like an artist. The main thing is to be BRAVE and have FUN!

Thank you for the lesson, Vincent. You are the bravest painter of all. I have learned so much from you.

Chat About Art

Vincent was a lonely man. People laughed at his paintings. They couldn't see that the strange man with the yellow beard was one of the greatest artists who ever lived. Read *Camille and the Sunflowers* and chat about tolerance and prejudice and the way in which some people are "outsiders"...

Self-portrait with a Straw Hat

In what ways are people different? How would you relate to someone who was different from you? Would you be kind to them like Camille, or would you be a bully? Perhaps that person has hidden abilities that we do not notice because they look different or have a different background or way of talking.

Search for portraits by these great artists:
VAN GOGH, GAUGUIN, REMBRANDT, LUCIAN FREUD
FRIDA KAHLO, ERNST KIRCHNER.

Make a Funky Junk Sculpture with Picasso

You will need: a collection of unused objects and materials, string or wire, strong glue, a basic tool kit if available, and lots of imagination.

My name is Sylvette. Picasso called me "the girl with the ponytail."

Guess where I am? I'm inside Picasso's studio. He has promised to show me how to build my own sculpture. While we're waiting, we'll have a look around....

Picasso is a genius. If you don't believe me, see if you can find some of the work he did when he was a young boy.

The best thing about Picasso is he is so inventive — he is never scared of experimenting with wild ideas.

Although he is very rich, Picasso loves junk. He doesn't throw anything away. Look at these fantastic junk sculptures....

A bull's head made from a bicycle seat and handlebars

A baboon made with two toy cars for a face

These sculptures are called objets trouvés, which is French for "found objects".

Who's in my studio? Ah-ha! It's my friend, Sylvette. Don't be shy. Come and meet my little dog, Lump. Would you like me to show you how to build your own junk sculpture?

Making junk sculptures is great fun, and it's kind to the planet, too.
First we need a junk collection. Here you are, Sylvette, take this bucket and see what you can find....

WARNING

NEVER TOUCH ANYTHING SHARP OR DANGEROUS. AVOID BROKEN GLASS AND DO NOT OPEN JARS OR BOTTLES IF YOU DON'T KNOW WHAT'S INSIDE. IF IN DOUBT, ASK AN ADULT.

That's very good, Sylvette.
We can join things together with wire,
string, or glue. Ask an adult to help
with screws or nails. There are no rules —
you can use plaster and fabric, too.
If it doesn't work
right away,
you can pull bits off
and change them.

SECRET:
Let it all change.
Whether you are
painting, making
sculptures, or even writing
stories, it's very important to let things
change and grow while you work.
Pull bits off, stick new bits on —
and don't worry.

You can also make a hanging
sculpture called a mobile...

Or make a 3-D junk painting by
sticking objects onto a board.

I'm pouring
sand into the
wet glue.

Chat About Art

Pablo Picasso started making art when he was a small boy. He became one of the most famous and richest artists who ever lived, and he was never afraid to invent new ways of making art. In his life, he created more than 30,000 amazing paintings, sculptures, drawings, and prints.

In 1954, Picasso met Sylvette David, "the girl with a ponytail". Sylvette was a very shy girl, but Picasso helped her to become an artist herself, and now she works every day in her own studio.

Picasso was a genius, but do you think a genius is born that way, or can anyone become a genius? Read *Picasso and the Girl with a Ponytail* and talk about genius. Does it help if people praise what you do? Have a look at the last secret in this book: being confident.

Woman with Baby Carriage

Search for sculptures by these great artists:
PICASSO, RODIN, ANTHONY GORMLEY,
BARBARA HEPWORTH, GIACOMETTI, HENRY MOORE.

Leonardo's Mad Marvelous Machines

You will need: large sheets of paper, brown paint (or some very strong tea!), pens or drawing materials, and lots of crazy ideas.

Perhaps it's time I showed you how to make your own marvelous machines.

I'm sorry, Leonardo, I was looking at your plans for a flying machine.

Your invention might make the world a better place, or it might be something silly just for fun. I designed this war machine, but perhaps you could design a machine to stop war?

SECRET:

I don't mind Zoro peeping in my notebooks. He won't be able to read my ideas because I use a TOP SECRET CODE.

Look, I have used "mirror writing" — I write back to front...

so you can only read my writing in a mirror.

Of course, you can draw on any paper you can find, but it's fun to make your paper look like old parchment. The easiest way is to use masking tape to stick a sheet of cartridge paper on a board. Mix up a yellowy-brown wash or use strong tea. Dab it all over the paper with a sponge or brush.

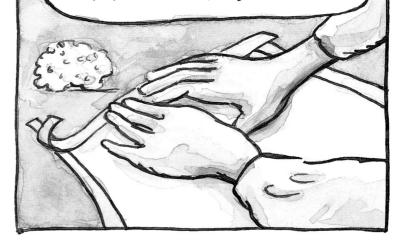

While the "parchment" is drying, take a notebook and have a brainstorming session. What kind of machine would you like to see?

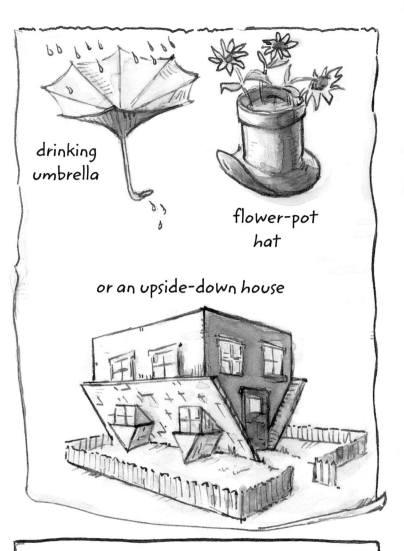

drinking umbrella

flower-pot hat

or an upside-down house

Could you design something which would make life easier for babies? For parents? For people with disabilities? For teachers or twins?

Just let your imagination go! Now it's time to sketch out your invention on your parchment. Start in pencil so you can erase and make changes. When you are ready, draw over the pencil line with a pen. If you use brown ink it will look just like an original Leonardo! Let's see what Zoro has invented. ... My goodness! A flying bicycle! Come back, Zoro!

Chat About Art

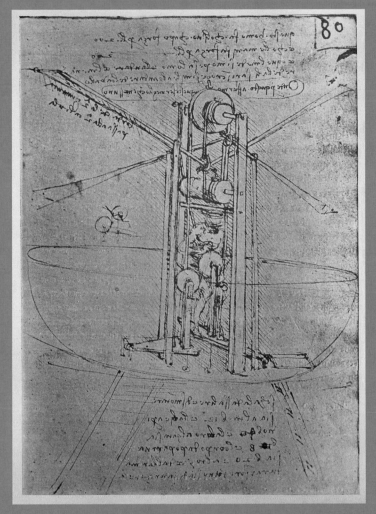

Studies of Flying Machine

Leonardo da Vinci was born in 1452 (500 years before Picasso). This great genius had the amazing idea of making a drawing of every object in the world — of course he didn't succeed, but perhaps the Internet has come a bit closer to making his dream come true. Leonardo lived during the Italian Renaissance. Renaissance means "born again," and this was a time of many wonderful inventions and great art.

Are we living in a Renaissance now?

Perhaps this is a Technological Renaissance (computers and robots) or a Green Renaissance (ecology and alternative energy)?

What do you think people will say about our world in 500 years' time? Read

Read Leonardo and the Flying Boy, and search for amazing inventions by these artists: LEONARDO DA VINCI, W. HEATH ROBINSON, RENÉ MAGRITTE, M.C. ESCHER, JEAN TINGUELY.

Art in Action with Degas

You will need: some self-drying modeling material – there are many types available, such as "Das," "Plasticine," and "Sculptamould"; alternatively, make papier maché with shredded newspaper soaked in diluted PVA adhesive. You will also need wire, such as coat-hanger wire or sculptors' aluminum armature, rubber gloves, and lots of patience.

My name is Marie. I was the little dancer who posed for Degas. Today Degas will teach me how to make my own sculpture of a figure in action.

Degas is often bad tempered, so I hope he won't be grumpy today.

Humph! Who is disturbing me? Oh, it's my friend, Marie.... Yes, I remember — we are going to make models of figures in action.

Humph! Let's see now... you could make a dancer, of course... or a football player or an athlete of any kind. First of all, we need some reference material. Find some really exciting photos of people in action.

Or you could look on the Internet.

Humph! I've never heard of the Internet...

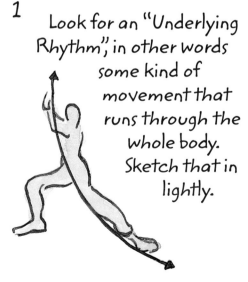
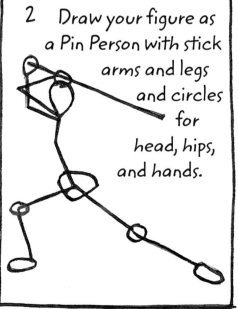

SECRET:

In 2002, a team of scientists at the National Gallery in London took an X-ray of my sculpture of the Little Dancer. They discovered my secret — I made armatures out of wire, pieces of wood, tin lids, bottle tops, and even old paint brushes! I was making it up as I went along.

You can make an armature with sticks or bendy wire. Have a good look at your reference photo and make a Pin Person like the one in your drawing.

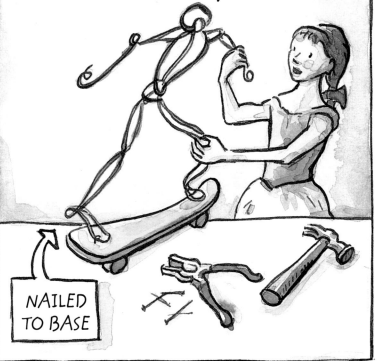

NAILED TO BASE

I often make my sculptures in wax, and I even stick on real fabric or hair, but there are all kinds of materials you can use to make sculptures — the easiest is Plasticine, but it might get squashed. My favorite material is papier maché, and it's almost completely free! Papier maché is easy to make....

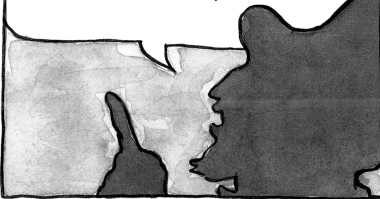

PAPIER MACHÉ

1 Tear thin paper such as newspaper into strips. (You may want to wear rubber gloves.)

2 Mix two parts white glue (PVA) with one part water and stir.

3 Dip paper strips in glue and pull off excess glue with fingers. You can store glue in a jar or a sealed plastic box.

28

Chat About Art

Degas was passionate about ballet. He made hundreds of images of dancers. Do you have a passion for something? It might be dancing, sport, writing, singing, or travel. Read *Degas and the Little Dancer* and discuss how you could use your passion to inspire your art. Is it better when people have a job which is something to do with their passion?

Little Dancer of Fourteen Years

Search for Movement in Art by these great artists:
DEGAS, UMBERTO BOCCIONI, JACKSON POLLOCK, GEORGE BELLOWS, BRIDGET RILEY, BALLA.

ONE LAST THING

When you draw or make a model of a figure, you can tell if the proportions are correct by using the FRANKENSTEIN TEST! Imagine your drawing or sculpture coming to life and walking around the room. Would the proportions look right or have you created Frankenstein's Monster with a huge head or tiny legs? Aaargh! Run for it!

Matisse's Cool Color Creations

You will need: lots of sheets of thick paper (construction paper is fine), a set of bright water-based paints such as acrylics or poster paints, a large decorator's brush, good-quality scissors, glue sticks or PVA adhesive, and some music to inspire you!

Your shapes can overlap, and they can touch each other. Don't forget that the spaces between your shapes make shapes too! You will find that by adjusting the shapes a little, your composition will get better and better.

HAVE ANOTHER LOOK AT VINCENT'S TIP: JIGSAW SHAPES ON PAGE 10.

SECRET:
A good composition will work upside-down or back-to-front! Look at any great painting upside-down or in a mirror and you will see that the composition is just as strong. Get into the habit of doing the same thing with your own work.

But how do I choose my colors?

Use your instincts, Monique. Which colors work well together? Try putting "opposite" or "complementary" colors together. For example: Blue/Yellow, Green/Purple, Red/Turquoise.

Groovy, baby!

Now I am carefully sticking my shapes in place. I marked the position with a pencil so I know exactly where they go. I love making cool compositions with Matisse!

Chat About Art

Disability — many artists had some kind of mental or physical impairment: Degas and Monet suffered from visual impairment, Matisse spent the last part of his life in a wheelchair, and Van Gogh had serious mental problems. Read *Matisse, King of Color*, and talk about the way in which disabilities affected some great artists' work. Perhaps their work would not have been so exciting if they were "able-bodied."

The Codomas, plate X1 from "Jazz"

Search for cool colors by these artists:
MATISSE, DERAIN, KANDINSKY, BONNARD.

ONE LAST WORD

If you want to try something really interesting, you can make pictures that describe a feeling — for example, red spiky shapes may look ANGRY. Smooth blue shapes may appear CALM. What happens if you use only dark colors — or just light colors? Have fun finding out.

Monet's Wild Wet Watercolors

You will need: some sheets of thick paper (cartridge paper or proper watercolor paper is best), a set of watercolor paints and brushes, jars of water, a soft cloth or paper towels, and a lovely view!

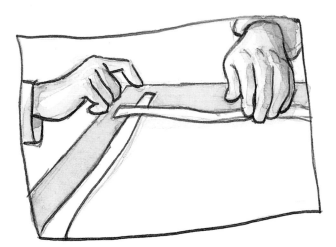

1   First, fix your paper onto a board.

2   Then make the paper slightly damp all over.

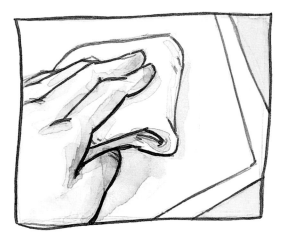

3   Use paper towels or a rag to dry off any excess water.

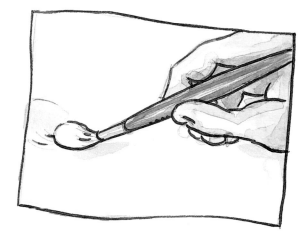

4   Now paint a strip of very wet yellow. This is called a wash of color.

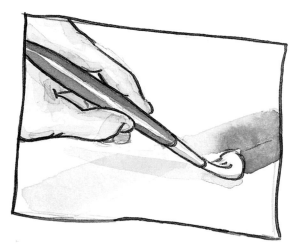

5   Next to it paint a strip of very wet red.

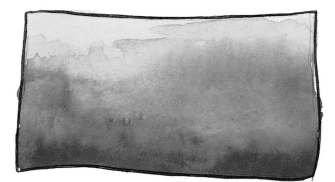

6   Let the two colors touch and you will see they blend to make a beautiful orange.

TIP: Keep your colors clean. Have one jar of water for washing brushes and another jar of clean water to mix with your paints.

Make your paper slightly damp all over and start to paint very freely. Begin with the sky or the background, and keep your colors very pale to begin with — so mix in lots of clean water.

You may feel a little out of control, but don't panic! With watercolors, there is nothing better than a HAPPY ACCIDENT!

After a while, the paper begins to dry a little, so now you can add some details in the foreground that will be sharper and darker.

When your painting is really dry, you can even draw into it with pencils, crayons, or pens.

That was a beautiful painting, Julie.

Thank you, Mr. Monet. You taught me to go with the flow.

Chat About Art

The Rose Path at Giverny

As he got older, Monet's eyesight became very poor and everything seemed blurry. But it didn't stop him from painting. Some of the last pictures he made are blurry too, but they are full of color and atmosphere and many people think they were the best paintings he did. Do you think paintings need to be "realistic" like photographs, or are you more interested in "abstract" qualities like atmosphere or expression?

ONE LAST THING: Seeing like an alien

If you see the same street or the same view every day, you may think it isn't very interesting. But the things which artists paint are just ordinary too — van Gogh painted old chairs and a pair of boots, Monet painted trees and skies — they just learned to see the beauty in ordinary things. So here's a great trick… Imagine you have landed on this planet from outer space. You are seeing things for the first time! Every street is strange, every tree is extraordinary, and what about those weird things called people? When you see like this, you realize that our "ordinary" world is amazing. If you look at it in this way, even a crumpled piece of paper is as astonishing as mountains covered in snow! You are looking at the world with an artist's eye!

Read *The Magical Garden of Claude Monet*,
and search for atmopheric paintings by these great artists:
MONET, TURNER, CASPAR DAVID FRIEDRICH, EDVARD MUNCH.
Also look at the lovely art by Julie's mother, Berthe Morisot.

Cézanne's Charcoal Challenge

You will need: some sheets of strong paper (construction paper is fine), some sticks of charcoal, which you can buy at any art store, an old rag or paper towels, a hard plastic eraser, and some hair spray!

My name is Paul. I would like you to meet my father. He is called Paul too — Paul Cézanne, the painter of mountains.

It's very early in the morning, but I think we'll find him up here. This is where he comes to work and get away from people.

I have to warn you that some people get a shock when they see my father. You see, he is very tall and he looks a little wild. But don't be scared — he's really very kind, and he has promised to show us how to draw with charcoal.

There he is... There's my father sitting by his fire.

Ah, it's Paul, my little apple boy. I have saved you some breakfast.

41

Look at this apple, Paul. How can you tell it is round?

Hmm... well, the light shines on one side, and the other side is in shadow.

Exactly! It's the light which makes it look solid or 3-D.

With charcoal, you get a whole range of tones. Use shading to make your shadows.

If you want, you can lightly blend the tones with a finger or a rag.

Use the tip of an eraser to put in highlights. Now your drawing begins to look real.

You can spray your drawing with hair spray to stop it from smudging. That's wonderful, Paul. Tomorrow we'll try a charcoal portrait.

I love working with charcoal.

Yes, Paul, but here is something you won't like so much....

A good wash with soap and water!

Chat About Art

Green Apples

Cézanne was inspired by nature. He spent much of his life walking and painting in the wild mountains of Provence. If the weather was poor he would often paint apples or portraits in the studio.

Read *Cézanne and the Apple Boy* and discuss the importance of nature in your own life — what is the wildest place you have ever visited? Have you ever been completely alone in nature?
How did you feel?

Search for images of nature by these great artists:
CÉZANNE, TURNER, GEORGIA O'KEEFFE,
ANDY GOLDSWORTHY, CONSTABLE, FREDERICK E. CHURCH.

If you are serious about being an artist, you should set up your own art cupboard where you can keep all your materials. Or you could have an art bag like my rucksack. I carry it wherever I go, and it's full of paints, sketchbooks, brushes, charcoals, rags, and everything I need to create a work of art.

LAURENCE ANHOLT'S SECRET

I hope you enjoyed making your own masterpieces. I have one final tip, and it's really the most important one of all... BE CONFIDENT!

Imagine you are starting a drawing. Suddenly a friend comes over and starts to boss you around and laugh at your work — "What are you doing?" they say. "Your drawing is terrible! I have a baby brother who is a better artist than you!"

Well, you wouldn't be very happy, would you? In fact you probably wouldn't feel like drawing at all after that.

In my experience, most of us have a bossy voice inside our heads... Do you? When you start a new project, do you hear a doubtful, negative voice telling you that you're no good? It's perfectly normal. The trouble is, if you want to be an artist (or anything else, for that matter), you need to be CONFIDENT! You need to trust your instincts. You can't even concentrate when your bossy friend is there.

So here's what to do...Tell the bossy voice (very politely) to go away. Tell them you are busy... and to come back later. THEN... change the bossy voice to the voice of your VERY BEST FRIEND...

"WOW! You are doing a painting! What fantastic colors! I think you must be the best artist I know!" Imagine what that would be like! You wouldn't worry at all if your best friend were there.

So that's all there is to it — talk to yourself in a kind way. Don't criticize yourself. Be your own best friend. And remember what Leonardo said:

"Anything is possible!"

ANHOLT'S ARTISTS

Collect all Laurence Anholt's brilliant books
about artists and the real children
who knew them.

Camille and the Sunflowers

Cézanne and the Apple Boy

Degas and the Little Dancer

Leonardo and the Flying Boy

Matisse King of Color

The Magical Garden of Claude Monet

Picasso and the Girl with a Ponytail

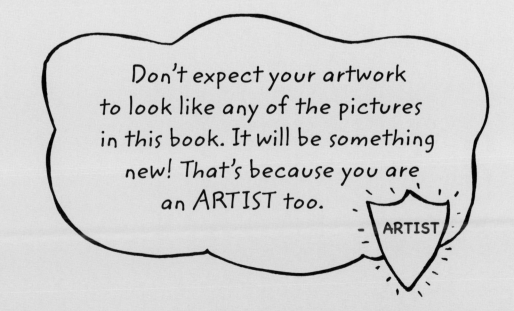

Don't expect your artwork
to look like any of the pictures
in this book. It will be something
new! That's because you are
an ARTIST too.

ARTIST